REMBRANDT and TITUS

ARTIST AND SON

———

Illustrations based on Rembrandt's work by Thomas Locker

Written by Madeleine Comora

Fulcrum Publishing
Golden, Colorado

For my father. —T. L.
For my mother and for Rahul. —M. C.

Library of Congress Cataloging-in-Publication Data

Comora, Madeleine.
  Rembrandt and Titus : artist and son / illustrations based on Rembrandt's work by Thomas Locker ; written by Madeleine Comora.
      p. cm.
  Summary: Titus, the son of famous artist Rembrandt van Rijn, tells how his father's life and work taught him about creativity and ways of seeing the world.
  ISBN 1-55591-490-X
  1. Rembrandt Harmenszoon van Rijn, 1606-1669—Juvenile fiction. [1. Rembrandt Harmenszoon van Rijn, 1606-1669—Fiction. 2. Artists—Fiction. 3. Creative ability—Fiction. 4. Fathers and sons—Fiction. 5. Netherlands—History—17th century—Fiction.] I. Title: Rembrandt and Titus. II. Locker, Thomas, 1937- ill. III. Title.
  PZ7.C7347Rem 2005
  [Fic]—dc22

                          2004030229

Printed in China
0 9 8 7 6 5 4 3 2 1

Design: Nancy Duncan
Editorial: Robert C. Baron, Katie Raymond
Cover image: Thomas Locker

Fulcrum Publishing
16100 Table Mountain Parkway, Suite 300
Golden, Colorado 80403
(800) 992-2908 (303) 277-1623
www.fulcrum-books.com

REMBRANDT AND TITUS

ARTIST AND SON

Illustrations based on Rembrandt's work
by Thomas Locker

Written by Madeleine Comora

Fulcrum Publishing
Golden, Colorado

The north light streamed into the studio while my father, Rembrandt, painted my portrait.

"Sit very still, Titus," he said, "and I will paint you the way I see you."

I heard the ships' bells echo along the canals of Amsterdam as I watched him brush a layer of oil paint onto the canvas. It was then that I decided to write this story about my father and how I learned to see the world through his eyes.

My father was born in Leiden. He didn't want to work in a flour mill like his father or go to the university. He wanted to be an artist.

When my father was only fourteen, he studied with a local painter. After several years, he mastered his craft and came to Amsterdam, where dikes held back the sea and the smell of salt water and malt ale filled the air. It was the center of the Dutch art world.

The city was booming. Merchants, craftsmen, and painters were everywhere.

In just a few years, my father became the most popular and successful artist in the city. He married my mother and bought a big house on Breestraat, the broad street, near Saint Anthony's Canal. In his studio upstairs he painted many portraits of her.

Soon their house was filled with students eager to learn my father's way of painting. They also wanted to know how he did his etchings. They were like no one else's, and people all over the world wanted to buy them.

"Everything was perfect then," he told me. He wished things could have stayed that way. But not long after I was born, my mother became ill and died.

I began understanding the way my father saw the world when we were out walking one day. On the bridge over the Amstel River we watched ships sailing south. The wind blew thick white clouds over the flat countryside.

"Look at the clouds reflecting the sunlight, Titus, and the shadows they cast on the water," my father said.

At the Singel Canal we saw a flower merchant laying out tulips in perfect rows. Then we saw a beggar, and my father immediately began to draw him. "Why do you want to sketch that ugly old man?" I asked.

"When you learn to see," he told me, "you will discover that there is beauty in everything."

There was a room in our house devoted to my father's collection of weapons, shells, and other rare things he used in his paintings. He took a helmet from his collection and painted a man wearing it. His painting captured the light reflecting off the helmet and gave it a rich, golden glow. He was fascinated by light set against the contrasting dark.

When I peered at the canvas up close, I saw only globs of paint.

He tugged at my sleeve. "The smell of the paint will bother you," he teased.

When I stood back, the globs of paint looked once more like real gold.

"Do you see how it glows from a distance, Titus?" he asked.

People flocked to my father's studio to have their portraits painted. They said he was the best painter in the city. He studied the expressions on their faces for a long time and noticed the smallest details, such as the shine on a nose or the way one eyelid was different from the other. He painted his sitters against a dark background, mainly illuminating their faces and hands. He caught subtle reflections and shadows that other painters paid no attention to. With a dab of white for the eye and an arched line for the eyebrow, he captured his subjects' spirits. His portraits seemed alive. When I looked at them, I felt I knew what the people were thinking and feeling.

A single eye painted by my father was more true to life than all the faces painted by other artists.

Sometimes my father painted groups of people. He was a natural storyteller, but he told his stories in unusual ways. Rather than lining everyone up in neat, still rows, he used his imagination and invented a dramatic moment. He depicted everyone in motion, some in the spotlight and others lost in a shadowy background. Somehow, using dark and light colors and rough and smooth paint, he unified all those portraits into one swirling image. Everyone in Amsterdam was amazed.

Most artists during my father's time didn't paint religious pictures because the Dutch didn't want art in their churches. But my father was fascinated by the characters in the Bible and felt inspired by them.

He discussed the Old Testament with a rabbi and used our Jewish neighbor as a model to paint Moses smashing the Ten Commandments. He highlighted his face and arms so they glowed with warmth, and gave him an expression that was filled with emotion.

People complained that the paint seemed too rough in places and looked unfinished. But my father told them, "A painting is finished when I have achieved my intention in it." He followed his own vision.

He also painted pictures based on the New Testament. Unlike some other artists, such as Michelangelo and Rubens, who depicted Christ as a muscular and handsome hero, my father painted him as an ordinary, suffering man you might see at the flower market or on any Dutch street.

My father was so deeply moved by one scene described in the New Testament that he included himself as one of the figures in the painting, not as a witness like other painters had done, but in the very center, helping to raise the cross.

In time, my father's work grew better, but the tastes of Amsterdam's art collectors changed. They wanted bright colors and smoothly painted pictures of ideal people and places, even if they weren't real.

My father painted people and places the way they were. He saw beauty and drama in everyday things.

When we walked along the riverbank one day, listening to the slap of water against a stone bridge, he pointed to the storm clouds and to the cottage roofs caught in a shaft of light. Later he recalled every detail of that moment's light in a painting. He used darkness to make the highlights more intense. He wanted your eye to search for things in the shadows, such as fishermen in their boats.

His style of painting was so unpopular that it became increasingly difficult for him to sell paintings. But my father stayed true to his vision.

My father always spent more than he earned and soon he began to run out of money. He still collected art and other rare objects, even though he couldn't afford them. As I grew older, he fell deeper and deeper into debt. Finally, he had to sell our big house along with his collection. I was sad to see him lose all the things he loved.

We moved to a smaller house on the Rozengracht Canal. Our housekeeper, who was like a mother to me, helped me start a company to manage my father's business affairs.

My father didn't change the way he painted. I often watched him paint pictures of himself with the same honesty that he painted other people. He wasn't interested in flattering himself. He was trying to understand himself in order to understand the world.

Each day I continued to take care of business so that my father was free to paint. He began to paint like never before. The surfaces of some of his pictures became rougher as he piled on thick coats of paint in the highlights. In other paintings he daringly finished some sections with fine details, contrasting them with parts that were hardly painted at all and could barely be seen.

He loved paint and made it do amazing things. His shadows were deeper and more vibrant, and the wonderful light on his subjects seemed to make them glow from within. He painted many religious pictures, as well as imaginary images of famous people from the past. Some of these became his most meaningful portraits.

My father kept on painting and trying to understand the world. One day he looked at his reflection in the mirror and painted his own portrait—the way he saw himself. When I looked at it, I saw an old man who had known both great joy and sorrow in his life. And I saw something else: he had captured his spirit. He was a truly creative human being.

I listened to the bells ringing on the ships sailing out to sea as sunlight streamed through the leaded glass windows, flooding the studio with golden light. I have learned to see through my father's eyes. I think he is the greatest artist that has ever lived.

Rembrandt van Rijn was born on July 15, 1606, in Leiden, Netherlands, where, during the seventeenth century, a flowering in the arts produced some of the greatest masterpieces the world has ever known. There are some moments in history when there has been this kind of freedom, and Rembrandt lived in such a time.

After eighty years of conflict with their Spanish rulers, the people of Holland and the allied provinces expelled the Spaniards in the late 1500s. The Golden Age of the Netherlands then began. The Dutch courageously built dikes to hold back the sea and pumped water into canals using windmills to create rich farmland. They formed a society that valued religious tolerance, imagination, and great achievement. Instead of the church or a royal court, a rising middle class of prosperous bankers, merchants, and traders became the patrons of the arts. The excellence of craftsmanship was astounding. Even second-rate painters demonstrated superb skills, and a few masters went even further. Rembrandt, already an accomplished master at the age of nineteen, dared to use the freedom that existed during his life to soar to new realms and depths of human experience.

In 1631 he moved to Amsterdam, a fast-growing world trade center. He married Saskia van Uylenburgh, and in 1641 Titus was born, the only one of their four children to survive infancy. After Saskia's death in 1642, Rembrandt raised Titus in the house with the help of their housekeeper, Hendrickje Stoffels. By the time Titus was fifteen, Rembrandt had fallen into so much debt that he had to declare bankruptcy and take on a more humble lifestyle. He continued to paint with uncompromising integrity. "A pious character values honor above wealth," he once wrote beneath a sketch. Even though his painting style eventually fell out of favor with the Amsterdam art community, he was one of the most revered artists of his century.

Titus didn't show the same talent at drawing and painting as his father, but as a boy he drew and painted many things, including the family pets. Before Rembrandt's death, Titus fell ill with the plague that swept through Holland and died at the age of twenty-seven. A year later, in 1669, Rembrandt died at the age of sixty-three.

Rembrandt's paintings have been studied for generations. To this day, his technique remains, in large part, a mystery. At times appearing chaotic, often with no trace of a brush or palette knife, the areas, or "passages," in his paintings have left artists and historians in awe. Many have said that his rich, varied, and seemingly effortless handling of thick paint, called impasto, along with his mastery of shadow and light, were the result of a lifetime of knowledge, experience, and passion. One has only to look at a self-portrait done late in life to see that he especially reveled in highlights, in swirls of paint where he put down thick daubs of white that reflected light, creating a luminosity so characteristic of his work. The faces he painted seem to be alive, while the hard-edged portraits by many other artists of his time appear frozen and lifeless in comparison. In his passionate pursuit of light and rich color, Rembrandt found meaning in the here and now, in the tragic glory of human existence, and in the world around him.

The fascination with and love of his work for more than four centuries has led to Rembrandt being called a genius, an alchemist, and even a sorcerer, but, above all, one of the greatest painters ever known to the world.

SOURCES

Rembrandt's paintings and etchings on which the illustrations are based:

Cover: Original painting by Thomas Locker, inspired by
Ruisdael and Meindert Hobbema.
Title Page: *Self-Portrait*, 1640, oil on canvas.
Page 5: *Titus at His Desk*, 1655, oil on canvas.
Page 7: *The Windmill*, an original painting by Thomas Locker,
based on an etching.
Page 9: *The Prodigal Son*, 1635, oil on canvas.
Page 11: *The Beggar*, an original painting by Thomas Locker,
based on an etching.
Page 13: *Man with a Golden Helmet*, 1650, oil on canvas.
Page 15: *Portrait of Jan Six*, 1654, oil on canvas.
Page 17: *The Night Watch*, 1642, oil on canvas, and also
based on one of Rembrandt's drawings.
Page 19: *Moses with the Tablets of the Law*, 1659, oil on canvas.
Page 21: *The Elevation of the Cross*, 1633, oil on canvas.
Page 23: *The Stone Bridge*, 1637, oil on panel.
Page 25: Original painting by Thomas Locker of Rembrandt
painting his self-portrait with Titus and Hendrickje.
Page 27: *Aristotle Contemplating the Bust of Homer*, 1653, oil on canvas.
Page 29: Original painting by Thomas Locker of Rembrandt with windmill
behind him, based on his last self-portraits.
Back Cover: *Titus at His Desk*, 1655, oil on canvas.

BIBLIOGRAPHY

Bailey, Anthony, *Rembrandt's House* (Boston and London: Houghton Mifflin Co., 1978).

Rosenberg, Jakob, *Rembrandt: Life and Work* (New York: E. P. Dutton, 1968).

Schama, Simon, *Rembrandt's Eyes* (New York: Alfred A. Knopf, 1999).

Van Den Boogert, Bob, and Museum Het Rembrandthuis, *Rembrandt's Treasures*
(Amsterdam: B. V. Waanders Uitgeverji Pub., 2000).

Van De Wetering, Ernst, *Rembrandt: The Painter at Work*
(Amsterdam: Amsterdam University Press, 2000).